PLACES, PLEASE, ACT ONE

Poems around and about theatres

WARREN KLIEWER

Foreword by
RAYLENE HINZ-PENNER

ISBN: 978-1-990827-15-0

What is an ideal rehearsal period?

"Two more weeks."

MAURICE MAETERLINCK

CONTENTS

FOREWORD

RAYLENE HINZ-PENNER

While I was teaching American literature to college students, I always loved imagining the great modern American poet, William Carlos Williams, a medical doctor with a passion for writing poetry, scribbling on his prescription pad while awaiting his next patient. The result was a series of classic short poems just the size of a prescription pad. A passionate poet writes on what is available, about life as it is being lived. A poet carries the thought of a poem all the while doing their prescribed work, waiting for the moment to spill the words onto the page and see if the language will gather the thoughts as imagined.

So too Warren Kliewer's collection of "poems around and about theatres," as he subtitles this collection, *PLACES, PLEASE, ACT ONE.* Kliewer writes the world wherein he spent his life and love, gathering his experiences into poems to offer a reader the intimacies of theatre life, even including his personal angst and insecurities as the actor/poet recounts his life "around and about theatres." His subjects range as broadly as Kliewer's vast experience and interests: summer stock theatre, set design, the coach in rehearsal, stretching the proceeds of a Saturday night box office to cover costs, the experience of a curtain call, reading fan mail, auditioning, the out-of-work actor, an explication of stage fright, the aging actor poking around in a once-great-and-now-abandoned theatre house, analysis of a resume, the actor's backstage mental preparations, and bar talk among the cast after the show. Before the final poem, Kliewer has drawn a reader into the wit, wisdom, and psychological weight of a life in the theatre as only poetry can with its reliance upon specific details and precise experience.

In his own introduction to this collection of poems, Kliewer laments that there are not more poems about theatre; playwrights like Goethe, Molière, and T.S. Eliot wrote plays in *verse*, of course, a different thing than writing poems about theatre. A lifelong poet himself while he lived out his vocation on the stage, Kliewer believed that actors and poets should have a closer alliance, thus this collection of poems whose subject, he notes, "is the private life of a public art form." That private life of theatre could only be shared in poetry. Indeed, that is the charm of the collection. It offers Kliewer a chance to be personal, even intimate, as a poem demands, to explore the "emotional knots," he suggests, "fumblingly untangled for the time being." Kliewer echoes here, in his way, Robert Frost's definition of poetry as a "momentary stay against confusion."

The poems are arranged into five sections: Apprenticeship, Dilemmas, Tributes, The Search, The Work. They read as one might expect of poems by a dramatist about the theatre, as if they were written to be heard, to be performed; these are performance poems. A reader begs from the first line of each poem to hear it on the tongue of a great reader (better yet, actor). That is, the spoken phrase leaps off the page, from the first poem, "A Story About Beginnings" (emphasis on "story"). "A Story" is Kliewer's recollection of his stage debut as a six-year-old ("hush,/the story is about to begin"), and the word "hush" is more than a stage direction. This poem is about silence and reflects the wisdom of the man, not the boy who will only recognize years later the power of the theatre: the "expectant silence" of the audience that had charmed him even as a six-year-old.

Indeed, in this first poem Kliewer's definition of a poem is reflective of the one laid down by the great English Romantic poet William Wordsworth when he defined poetry as "the spontaneous overflow of powerful feelings" arising from "emotion recollected in tranquility." In another childhood poem set in the grape arbor of summer, no doubt in Kliewer's hometown of Mountain Lake, Minnesota, the children feel their way into impromptu theatre to tell a story of "sailing over the roiling waves to the New World!" When someone's mother comes with lemonade just as the actors are on the brink of a bloodbath, the poet wonders, harking back from the tranquil time of pensive adulthood, whether there might be a "boy-instinct that warns us when to pull back." He ends the poem with the actor's psychological wisdom reflecting on the six-year-old: "It takes a man a lifetime/to learn when not to [pull back]." This same reflective tone is evidenced throughout the collection. In a poem on lessons for summer stock applicants, the poet advises that what is on stage is unreal; "only the ideal is real" — even as he knows the apprentices will forget. "We all do." To forget is to survive. The poem ends in the poignant and mature voice of the aging actor: "It's winter now. These poems are an attempt to remember."

Often, the poet remembers as he reflects on the interplay between the harsh realities and mundane requirements of making theatre, and the ethereal, ideal dreams of the creative team."REHEARSING THE SUNLIGHT" begins with an epigraph-like two lines: "More light,"/said Goethe on his deathbed." The rest of the poem details the lighting designer's attempts to make do with overloaded circuits as he tries to create enough light on stage for the desired sunrise. In the end Kliewer's longing for a lighted stage merges with Goethe's desire where the poem began: "I crave brightness!/ So did the poet begging for light/who knew how much light costs/in overloaded circuits." Those final lines contain a fine example of how Kliewer works toward wit and wisdom in these poems--with juxtaposition and punditry--to "overload" the language with implication. Surprise, we know, is the central requirement all readers demand of poetry. How much light does cost! And yes, there is the matter of overloading our own circuits with the brightness we crave.

Kliewer's poems in this collection even attest to his wrestling with the everyday moralities in the choices required of him in theatre. Just as a college instructor experiences inner turmoil over the morality implied by the canon she chooses to teach in a literature course, Kliewer reviews his line-up of shows for the summer season--one about the Wednesday mistress, another "burdened/ with too much virginity" and yet another in which the hero "Finds his secretary's/Heart is in the right place--/Under her blouse. This helps him sell a lot of real estate." Purveying his line-up, Kliewer has a moment of pause before he ends his poem "THE LINE-UP" reflecting upon the "lines and lines of families" (that other lineup!) coming to attend the theatre. Other times the poet gets the last word (here, the last line) and the last laugh, as when a fan leaves the actor a note telling him to "drop dead" after he plays a villain. The actor's response in this poem: "I did drop dead in Act Three,/And now I'm going home." A reader is sometimes privy to wicked humor or come-uppance, even raw tenderness in the final lines of these poems. Kliewer is adept at poetry endings. Would we expect otherwise of one trained for the final stage line, subsequent bow, and applause?

Consequently, throughout this book of poems we find Kliewer attentive to the analogies and crossovers between the arts of theatre and the art of writing poems. He loves the word play that poems afford. "A CURTAIN SPEECH" cleverly uses the art of the pause, so significant on stage, now afforded by the poem's line break in this villanelle-like poem which repeats the line, "We played this evening's performance" in response to a playwright who didn't take keenly to the actors' ad libbing performance. The poet's final use of "played" references the actors playing on stage, playing the playwright. Indeed, in the Tributes section near the end of the book we find the poet playing poetry's elasticity with tongue-in-cheek words of praise to a certain actor as "raconteur . . . . recounter of every play he saw, recaller of every actor he knew since 1912." Throughout his work Kliewer indulges his love of word play: "A pause [Applause?] for Claude Kipnis, mime,/whose hands and feet spoke,/ whose ages-old whiteface/voiced new silence/until he found the stillness/that passes all understanding" ("IN TRIBUTE").

If I should commend this posthumous collection by Warren Kliewer for one attribute above all, it would be for its understanding of *timing*, which both on stage and in poetry becomes wit. It is that attribute referenced in one of the most poignant poems in the collection in the section titled "THE SEARCH." Both actor and poet know that timing is everything. "DEAR SIR/MADAM" begins "Enclosed please find my resume—" whereupon the actor proceeds to explain what is listed in his resume (only the three shows which told the truth). More importantly, the actor details what is not listed in the resume, to wit, his life. Because of the vicissitudes of timing, he will not list "those that fooled/us all because the politics were right/ that moment and never again, nor those that missed/completely, a month too soon or a year too late." In theatre, as in the writing of poetry, timing, one's life, one's resume, is everything: "To make a life in the theatre, move on./No used solutions. Burn your old promptbooks. Smother/your tricks and triumphs. Each birth is a new one. That leaves us with wide margins. Do feel free/to use them for your own thoughts." Surprising as advice from a resume writer, it is clearly the philosophy of Warren Kliewer the actor writing his resume in this collection of poems, telling his life. We see it in the poem's last line, "Do feel free/to use [the margins] for your own thoughts. –Most sincerely." No doubt this is why Kliewer chose poetry to share his truths about theatre. Poetry demands that the reader share in the experience of writing the poem in a way not unlike the relationship between actor and audience. Readers of poems must be willing to write their own resumes in the margins. The poet must leave room for a reader to bring their own presence to bear on the poem, to work alongside, bring their own life, whatever their differing experience, to write the poem in the margins in cooperation with the poet. This, Warren Kliewer understood, "Most sincerely."

The final poem in the collection, "Act Three—The Silence" is chilling in the way it presages Warren Kliewer's untimely death as he anticipates a new silence different from the silence that awed the actor as a six-year-old in the first poem in this collection. That expectant silence of an eager audience or reader had allowed this actor to fill the room with his own presence both in the theatre and in the way a poet fills the page with the details of his theatre life. In this final poem Kliewer worries about earning his way to the third act's silence, the "hush and lull." The poet admits that he is sweating off stage thinking about Act Three, and therefore, "emptying/to become/someone else/I care about,/ . . . on the way to peace." The poems in this collection are an elucidation of that emptying shared with the reader, beckoning them to go too in search of their own peace in life's drama. I invite you now to enter into the poetic yearnings and joys of the actor, director, and playwright, Warren Kliewer. *PLACES, PLEASE!*

Newton, KS
June 2024

INTRODUCTION: MAKING POEMS AND MAKING THEATRE

WARREN KLIEWER

Multitudes have made poems for music and about music, poems about paintings and sculptures and photos and Grecian pots, architectural poems about limestone wonders or the stores on Main Street or the falling-down barn on the family homestead, poems about dancers (usually seen from a distance and upwind), poems about poems or about poems-about-poems. All arts are suitable subjects for verse--all, that is, except theatre, which has evoked a mere handful of poetic efforts, and most of them by a single poet, Bertolt Brecht.

Surprising, isn't it? Poet-actor-playwright Ben Jonson played with supple verse on stage, but when he had Something Serious to say about the theatre, he put it in prose. Maybe he was our trendsetter. Goethe, Molière, and T. S. Eliot all made their plays in verse, and used prose for their Theory and Stuff.

"That's all right," the conventional wisdom would probably say. "As everyone knows, the theatre is so coarse, crude, crass, and physical that, like an overactive acid, it would corrode any container but leaden prose." I question this. Poets — a plucky lot, by and large — have not shied away from such hot choices as murder, revolution, incest, and drugged wooziness. Would anyone seriously contend that these are more dignified experiences than what an actress does when she merely loses her identity out in public for a couple of hours?

"Acting," a wise old actor once told me, "is like writing your name ... with your finger ... on the water." That melancholy thought has often made me wonder why there isn't a closer alliance between actors and poets, who could, if they would, take much from each other. Of course, they used to be the same person — before Homer: a splendid, unified time when it was a single mind-body both choosing the word and making it flesh. The actor-half embodied the ephemera of shifting emotions; the poet-half immortalized the transitory. It is no wonder that actors sometimes yearn for and inordinately admire the condition of poets who can bring the ever-changing physical finally to rest in words.

IN THE EYE OF THE BEHOLDER

Actors are in love with the
power of poets, who
précis a credo, a
lifetime, an epoch
in a quatrain;
in wonder at the wiliness
of lines of words,
Sandburg's looping and
snaking circularity,
Jeffers' roiling and
clashing against red rocks,
Grizzly McGrath's mythopoeic
long-line growling;
awed by all who can lavish
love on the language and
tame it; —
actors who swim in a
sea with no islands.

These poems have been written perhaps in honor of, but more likely in comradeship with, actors, directors, designers, technicians, and yes even producers. The final product of their labors — that which patrons buy tickets to see and critics get free tickets to grumble about — is not my subject. Rather, it's the work itself leading to the results. My subject is the private life of a public art form. These poems come from the ever-changing and inconclusive process.

Warren Kliewer in his Uncle Dan's Financial Tips

And these poems are all real — to the extent that anything in the theatre ever is. Each one comes from a theatre I actually worked in or a production I worked on or an emotional knot several of us in rehearsal somehow fumblingly untangled for the time being.

Secaucus, NJ, 1996
Warren Kliewer

APPRENTICESHIP

A STORY ABOUT BEGINNING

Once upon a time
upon a stage,
once upon a box
upon a platform
upon a stage,
a boy (that small) upon a box,
all eyes upon the boy,
silence upon the audience:
hush,
the story is about to begin.

The tale having ended,
the hands having clapped,
the lights burnt out,
the audience forgetting,
the boy forgotten,
the moment past,
the theatre closed,
the box tossed away:

The man--
years later
inside the theatre
upon the stage
within the pools of half-light--
heard again the silence
of an audience waiting
for the story to begin,
heard again the boy
(himself)
matching the expectant silence
with the most exultant
of silences.

SIX AND BEYOND

To begin
again
to simplify
to retreat to
the perfection
of being six years old
before one learned
the sin of comparing:

At six
ear and
voice are
clear
All tales are
true
even lies.

At fifty-six
all truths
are tales
They catch in
the two sides of
the mouth
The grinders
emit pulverized
product:

To begin again
seeking the
perfection of six
before one found
so many diversions
from one's
clear
self.

ADDITION

Two hands.

Bring them together?
Clap.
So one plus one equals clap.

Wave, wave?
Flying!
So one plus one equals bird.

What if I walk them across the floor
finger by finger?
One plus one equals Thousand Legs.

(Mathematicians of the world, quick,
bring lights!
Babies are dragging us down
into darkness!)

WHAT IF . . . AS IF . . .

A grape arbor, that's all we had
to work with, and only in the summers.
Springs, the walls were a mere pattern,
pipe-and-stick-work and leafless vines
writhing from posts like snakes
hung out to dry.
But summers, buds grew into leaf flaps
closing in the darkness
of a place apart
we could make into what
it needed to be.

Let's call it "The Golden Hind."
I'm Sir Something and you're Sir What?
Drake. Raleigh.
Yeah, Sir Francis, Sir Walter.
What do we do?
Talk high-falutin'.
Why?
They's how they did it. I heard in school.
Where are we going?
Westward over the roiling waves to the New World!
What will be our Fate?
The wind in our faces, the gales
Whipping the mainsail, shipwreck,
Hunger, thirst,
Bloody wars with brutal savages.
And so it came to pass.

At four o'clock, at the far edge
of the world, on the brink of a bloodbath,
someone's mother came around.
Saved with lemonade and cookies!
Or maybe there's a boy-instinct
that warns us when to pull back.
Must be. It takes a man a lifetime
to learn when not to.

SUMMER STOCK THEATRE

A Handbook for Apprentices

Summer stock theatre--the system by which an under-financed producer, using worried actors and harassed apprentices, whips together one show per week--is dying out. Big corporations are taking over.

Packages are touring. Theatres are resorting to sensible business methods. There aren't many places left for young people to apprentice.

Still, if you can find a summer stock job, take it. It will be a school for the soul, learning how to live in the midst of haste, weariness, and shoddiness. In that procession of dreary, mediocre days, there will be moments when you suddenly feel as if leaving home wasn't a mistake after all--moments of real theatre. In those moments you will suddenly know a painful irony of performing: that what is up there on that stage is unreal, and that only the ideal is real.

And then you'll forget again. We all do. Forgetting is a way to survive in summer stock.

It's winter now. These poems are an attempt to remember.

THE COMPANY MANAGER - JUNE FIRST

A one-bulb pilot light
Won't light this world.
Besides, this dusty platform
Is not the stage
That all the world is:
We do comedies and thrillers here.

The apprentices arrive tomorrow,
Unloading into the actors' lodge
Their bags and record players
And another year
Of college acting awards.

I'll have them hunt up
The other pilot light.
And sweep the stage.
Too bad you have to start
With bulbs and brooms.
Robert Edmond Jones didn't tell you
About bulbs and brooms.

THE SET DESIGNER REHEARSES HIS OPENING SPEECH

We do things quickly here.
Designed by Wednesday,
Built by Friday,
Painted Saturday,
Assembled from midnight
Till Sunday morning,
Finished Monday,
Touched up Tuesday,
The set looks . . .
Well, it looks a lot like last week's
And the weeks' before.
Can't help it--
Next week's another show.
We'll use the other color scheme.
We have two--
Each for every other show.

I had a dream last night.
We have a week to build
THE RIDE OF THE VALKYRIES:
Three mountains,
Valhalla,
Two castles,
A couple of sunsets,
24 horses for the Rhine maidens,
A pit for the orchestra,
719 new lighting instruments,
Expand the stage house 24 feet.
"This is your chance to express yourself,"
The director tells me.
"Finish it Monday.
Make it subtle."

COACHING THE INGENUE

Take the speech again, please.
Not the way I read it--
Find your own reading, dear.
Your own.
And sometime this August
After the season
Before the fall auditions,
Standing before a mirror,
Listening to your voice,
Watching the way your hands curve,
Remembering how your mind moves,
Wondering about your parents' childhood,
Hoping to hear the sounds of your heritage,
Ask what it means to be
Your own.

REHEARSING THE SUNLIGHT

"More light,"
said Goethe on his deathbed.
So did I
throughout the lighting rehearsal,
though all the circuits were overloaded.
Such a sunrise is worth it;
we'll take the risk,
patching and repatching
circuits between cues,
taping the circuit breakers down,
watching for flickers,
feeling the overheated boards,
hoping.
I crave brightness!
So did the poet begging for light
who knew how much light costs
in overloaded circuits.

THE LINE-UP

The line-up of shows:
The hero of the first week
Lets his wife go shopping
On Wednesday afternoons.
He has a Wednesday mistress
Who has a midweek mister.
Wednesdays are very busy.

The second week's heroine,
A matron and maiden,
Bored and burdened
With too much virginity:
She has a boss
Who has a wife,
Legal but large.
Maiden and man relieve each other
Of these odiousnesses.
Her digestion improves.

The hero of the third week
Sends his wife to Europe,
Moves into his office,
Works there every evening,
Finds his secretary's
Heart is in the right place--
Under her blouse.
This helps him sell a lot of real estate.

Sometimes I think about these shows
And worry about the line-up
At the box office--
These lines and lines of families.

SATURDAY NIGHT BOX OFFICE

Sold out.
299 seats times
$3.00
(minus
four broken ones)
equals
Saturday night.

Insurance
and gas bills
paid this week.
Cliff's gone,
so minus his salary
and monumental appetite
equals
profit.

Maybe I'd better pay
the phone bill
Monday
before we open
our annual
classic.

No, never mind.
The phone never
rings
when we play our
sole and single
annual
classic.

ANOTHER KIND OF FAN MAIL

A sheet of white, blue-flowered notepaper,
My name in rounded schoolgirl script on the
    outside,
Was pinned to the callboard.
Someone had stolen in at intermission.
Most ticketholders hesitate
At the double doors and the surly stage
    manager.
This one persisted.
I found the note as I left,
"Drop dead," it said.
Unsigned.

This happens every time I play a villain.
I wish I could meet her.
We'd have much in common:
My evil, her blue flowers.
Actors and children know
How artifice is real.
I did drop dead in Act Three,
And now I'm going home.

CURTAIN CALL

I heard a sob last night--just one--
in the pause between the last word
and the explosion of applause.
A person sitting in the second row,
whom no one knows,
unconnected,
a half-seen silhouette
just outside the light,
and then the sob:
I hear,
I know,
it's a man,
he is old,
he remembers,
he understands.
I bow to him.

DILEMMAS

PLAYWRIGHT IN A CROWD OF ACTORS WAITING TO AUDITION

Good God
So many out of work?
How can I support all of you with
My three-character fribble?
They must have food stamps for you people—
Or orphanages?
Why are you smiling at me?
I will not feel guilty for
Not supporting your families!
The producer came to this audition
In a Mercedes
And he wants to cut my
Third character.
God will punish him.
My wife sold her wedding ring to
Buy me a typewriter ribbon,
And now I can't look you in the eye,
You roomful of smiles,
You talent for hunger.
God, what wouldn't I do for
Five loaves and two fishes
Or even one
Hero.

BETWEEN ENGAGEMENTS

If I ever

                  (whenever)

work again

                  (if ever I can)

I will never

                  (please God)

ever complain about ten-hour rehearsals.

If I am ever cast again. . .

                (because only when acting
                            am I
                    what I am)

I will learn my lines on time.
I will declare the playwright a genius.
I will adore the leading lady
even when she steps on my lines.

Next time, next show:
    I will do everything the director demands.

                (for an actor not acting
                    is not an actor)

Delighted to shave my head, sir.
Change my name? Consider it done, sir.
Get taller, did you say? First thing tomorrow, sir.

On the day I go into rehearsal--

                        (I act,
                      therefore
                      I am)--

    I will address the stage manager as "Mister."
    I will vote in union elections
    and contribute to the Actors' Chapel.
    All my diseases will heal,
    the trains will run on time,
    and there will be World Peace.

STAGE FRIGHT

No one foresees it
It does not come
It was not there and then
it is there
Maybe it slipped in
through the cracks
in the floorboards
Or maybe we brought it in
clinging to our hair
like the smell of onions
and stale grease
Maybe it was always there--
here
always here--
but not yet released

How is it released
If someone had turned on
a burner and forgotten
to light a match
we'd smell it
This gas has no odor
no color
does not burn
or blow away

Maybe it frees itself
but no one notices
until an hour
or two days or a week
before opening night
Someone stops smiling
suddenly
Someone tries to take
a deep breath
and can't suddenly
Other throats catch
It terrorizes the dressing room

IMPROVISER

Why don't we try a
What if we put a
Wouldn't it be better to say

        a crush
        of reasons
        to avoid
        too soon
        committing
        never!
        I don't want to
        feel such
        hope
        less
        loss
        into who is this
        character
        I don't
        no

Wouldn't it be what if
Why don't I try it your way
which I don't like Sir and I hope

        you'll hold me back
        from
        crashing into
        your feelings which
        I think is best
        Your way
        As written
        Let's do it.

A SCRAP FALLEN FROM A DIRECTOR'S NOTEBOOK

no moving parts
inside this gem-
hard script's
solid surface
so no chinks
unbreakable
will endure
because no moving parts
to break
no moving crumbles
to clog cogs
no human parts for actors
to chip away
no human error to move
(O Perfect Playwright!)
me imperfect at my movable heart

ACTORS' CHOICES

Never
not whenever
ad lib
hesitating
impetuously--
NOW
or not at all.

FULL OUT
or fall back.
No fat on these feelings
no feelings about feelings--
FULL OUT
or go out.

Choices—
not driftings
yearnings
I.O.U.s to afterwords—
TAKE
not taken,
FULL OUT

NOW

TRIBUTES

THE (ONCE) MAJESTIC THEATRE

No lights in here now, and no glamor.
This stagedoor's held back its history
so long the hinges turned with a stammer

when I intruded. Blistering
green paint. Yes! Here the actors sat
preparing for the mystery,

so this room's used to silence. A cat?
black and on stage? Bad luck. But dead,
so not a spirit, not a threat,

I hope. And what more damage could
a cat do? Breathe: our future, the smell
of mold. "So are we all unmade,"

must have been said here once. A well
on stage? No, rot has dug new traps
in the stage floor: twelve mouths of hell,

beware the devils! Tattered flaps
of upholstery flutter where applause
swelled to the actors' triumphs. More gaps

than chairs now, velvet reduced to gauze.
Like the house that once knew Fiske and the Booths
And now holds only shreds of clues.

TO AN ACCIDENT-PRONE LEADING LADY

A sprained wrist--
how many times?
Laryngitis
(how many times?)
A fainting spell.
How many times? !
The symptoms are
visible
always
ensemble to her
pale complexion:
In her rehearsals
no one suffers
diarrhea or
halitosis.

O my lovely,
all of us in the third
quarter of rehearsals
anguish in
a dark night
of the soul.
But not with your grace,
Your Grace.

LESSON IN PERSPECTIVE

--for James Thompson, Scenic Designer

"Fast, that's how," growled the pedagogue
at ten wary students learning
how to draw in perspective.

"A line is a sweep of the arm, not fingers. The eye's
quicker than the brain. Think, and you'll never learn
how. To draw in perspective

size up the whole, then sketch, sketch, zip, zip,
DONE! No? Stack up ten sheets. I'll show you
how to draw in perspective

you dawdling dabblers. Ten seconds per drawing. Draw!"
Ten seconds later--"Next!"--and nine times more.
How to draw, in perspective

or flat, he never explained. He urged on his dawdlers,
trusting their eyes to find the vision he knew
how to draw in: perspective.

CURTAIN SPEECH

I can't even recognize it anymore!
They've taken it away from me!
-- From Interview with
a Playwright

We played this evening's performance--
Remarkably well, if I may say so--
In memory of our dear departed

Playwright, who's gone but not forgotten,
And whose French leave has been forgiven.
We played this evening's performance,

We rehearsed for him, we labored, anguished
In heart, in mind, in soul, in body,
In memory. Of our dear departed,

However, no news, not a word, note, memo,
Phone call, not even a Hallmark. So
We played this evening's performance,

Ad lib. A delicious show, not so? Yes,
Spontaneous changes are always healthy.
In memory of our dear departed

Author, we kept his title, some of
His language, the spirit of his playlet.
We played, this evening's performance,

Sweet variations on a theme by
The man without whom . . . what was his name?
We played this evening's performance,
In memory of our dear departed . . . ?

INTESTATE

for
Michael Lewis, Actor, 1930-1975

They
Could always find someone
Some goddamn producer
To send one of his scaly boxoffice bastards
To post the goddamn closing notice:
This time they found a goddamn doctor,
Ugly son of a bitch with red hair
Like my father's:
"Six months and out, you bastard,"
The M.D. said;
"Pay in advance."
I wrote him a bad check.
"You make it good
Or I'll put gravel in your catheter."
He will, too.
That's why they picked him.
One of my wives did it, rotten bitch,
Probably the one who ruined my voice
Making me yell at her,
Not the one who started me drinking.
I haven't been sober
Offstage since 1967.
Hangovers give you something to
Fight in the mornings
When there's no rehearsal.
God, was I peaceful
On stage.
No one's applauding now.
I'm plugged in like a patch panel--
They sent these rubber tubes down
To find my arms legs belly, and to crawl
Down my nose and
Up my crotch.

God I was good I was
On stage.
Up yours, Doc.
Never take checks
From actors
Who've gotten a closing notice.
God I might have been one
Of the great
Ones
now they've even
taken
away
my
last

ap
plause

IN TRIBUTE

Farewell to five
who have taken their last
calls:

Let us record
Jerome Collamore, actor and
raconteur, older than
the twentieth century,
recounter of every play he saw,
recaller of every actor he knew
since 1912,
who now has joined them
as history;

All honor to William DaPrato, actor,
whose overabundant nose
cast him forever as
Bill the Funnyface,
whose late luck led him into
his first graceful role
and lured him home for a nap
between shows,
where he slept through till
Judgment Day;

Peace, peace to Jonathan Chappell, actor
and scholar,
who raged
on stage,
who blustered with violence
on stage,
who was found at home with a
knife
in his heart and
silence
in his mouth;

All joy to Warrington Winters, actor,
who said yes and yes
to every part,
who said yes to ON BORROWED TIME,
who, at seventy-six, understood
that title.
"You know, don't you?," he would tell us,
"I'm a Seneca Indian."
Now he's in the ground
happily hunting for his next role.

A pause for Claude Kipnis, mime,
whose hands and feet spoke,
whose ages-old whiteface
voiced new silence
until he found the stillness
that passes all understanding.

"Exit,"
wrote The Playwright.
"You served the scene
well."

THE SEARCH

DEAR SIR/MADAM

Enclosed please find my resume--some twenty
years' work, five shows a year, not counting schools--
nor do I list readings, workshops, penny-ante
starved-budget shows, tryouts, nor those that fooled

us all because the politics were right
that moment and never again, nor those that missed
completely, a month too soon or a year too late.
That's why you see three shows on my list.

They told the truth, these three. Forget the others.
To make a life in the theatre, move on.
No used solutions. Burn your old promptbooks. Smother
your tricks and triumphs. Each birth is a new one.

That leaves us with wide margins. Do feel free
to use them for your own thoughts. -- Most sincerely,

AN EDUCATED ACTOR INTRODUCES A NEW
AUDITION PIECE

I'd like to do a monologue for you.

This cutting from the middle of a long scene
in the first act of a not-well-known play in
English verse adapted from a French novella,
prose, includes five lines from the scene in
the book which the playwright--God knows why
he did this, a mistake, believe me--omitted,
and adds a line or two, well, five, from the
novelist's never-before-translated notes now
available in THE COLLECTED NOTEBOOKS OF: et
cetera, a passage she cut from the *Urtext* of
her novel--another mistake--and an editorial
liberty, ten lines to be exact, or maybe not
more than a dozen, that I added to the scene
(i.e., this monologue) to build up climaxes,

as it were.

SQUARING-THE-CIRCLE SCENIC STUDIOS, INC.

Intimidated? Your designers demand the impossible?

Call the indomitable S-T-C. We work magic six days
a week; with T-squares, compasses, straight edges,
calipers, French curves, or freehand, any shape you
can name--circles, rectangles, ellipses, triangles,
ovoids, trapezia, heptahedrons, circles with square
corners--and shapes that don't have names yet:

doorways, windows, free-floating ceilings, columns,
sculptures, architraves, staircases in all periods,
elevators, structures not yet invented:

dungeons, castles, saloons, living rooms, churches,
street corners, barns, fields, kitchens, fountains,
clouds, mountains, glaciers; places your audiences
will want to move right into or get the hell out of
as you choose:

we'll build you Death Valley and the Sistine Chapel
back-to-back on a turntable if you can use them.

Free price quotes. The imaginable-impossible yours
at affordable prices.

ACTOR'S PREPARATION: CHECKLIST

Shakes, bends, stretches, sit-ups, running in place, heavy
heartbeat, sweat: Check.

Reread entire play, remark my entrances and exits,
review faulty memory: check.

Clean underwear: Check.

Callboard -- Initial sign-in sheet: Check.

Stage -- Armchair, easy chair, couch, right, left, center,
angled toward the lights: Check.

Backstage -- Handprops, pick up and reset, prop tables
right and left: Check.

Costume rack -- Rip in the vest sewed up: Check.

Dressing room -- Towel on the counter, water in the
glass, pencils left, brushes right, base at center,
tissues far left: Check.

Backstage -- Three deep breaths slowly: Check.

Onstage --
          Resolve: Check.
          Passion: Unchecked . . .

MAGIC TIME -- JIMMY RAY'S

This is the place. It's safe to
Confess your dreams:
      How are you doing my agent
      'S sending me up for a
      Part of it's already cast but
      Sang for O'Horgan who
      Called me back three times then
      Wanted a Scott voice I think
      It's almost a sure thing once I've
      Got three days on Love of Life
      buoy commercials are using
      Real people in the crowd
      Scenes from Coriolanus if you like
      Papp Shakespeare not my kind of
      Showcase but very good people who usually work
      For nothing but it's a good stage
      Managing credit and I was glad to
      See you've got another hemorrhoid commercial.
You're among friends here.
They'll make room for you at the bar.

PREPARING FOR REHEARSALS

To drive myself into
disciplined consciousness
in order to
voice:
            aaa eee iii ooo uuu:
a body:
            streeeetch reeeelax breeeeathe in/out:
and soul?

How?

to tune my dissonance?
They didn't teach me spirit-tautening
in acting school,

only the voicing
only the bodying forth.
An actor has no soul
at least in acting school
only the physics of harmonics
aaaa eee iiin uuuu out

GEORGE SPELVIN, UTILITY ACTOR

> No! I am not Prince Hamlet, nor was meant to be;
> Am an attendant lord, one that will do
> To swell a progress, start a scene or two. . .
> --T. S. Eliot

I can begin.
I can do.
I am able.
I am always present.
I always finish out the season.
I always learn my lines on time.
I never tear my costumes.
I make the stage seem full
Like a crowded room, a busy street corner,
A store during the lunch hour:
My: stage is as full as life.
My characters are full as if alive:
I play "The Second Man" or "The Corporal"
Or "The Bailiff" with one short scene,
And I give him such uniqueness, such character,
A place, a time, a history,
A wife, a child, a dog that has a name,
A taste for fancy food, someone to remember.
I am what the patrons come to the theatre for,
My love of the fullness of life
Half-hidden in the shadows upstage left of center.

THE WORK

PLACES, PLEASE, ACT ONE

Two minutes to curtain.
Well-wishers are silent now.
No one can help you make your entrance.
The blankness of an emptied mind.
Inhale, two, three. Exhale, two, three.
Sound, cue two: go.
Inhale, two, three.
Sound, cue two executed.
Music swells.
Lights, cue three: go.
I see too well, I hear
Whispers, my blood, everything.
And then,
Now!

STANDS FOR:

The actress carries a purse.
Therefore, she's a lady.

A busy cafe?
Set up two chairs and a table.

Change your hat
And you're a new man.

Stipple the flats with a sponge:
Texture!

Change the color of light:
Another time, another place.

A rock on stage means a rock,
Two rocks mean a mountain.

The audience's eye stops at the proscenium arch,
The outline of all they'll ever know.

The arch stands for limit.
Let them guess at what the rest means,
This movement in the shadows,
The mystery.

NOT NO-WORDS

(Pause.)
--Harold Pinter

I can say your words, Mr. Pinter,
But how about some help with the blanks?
I'm only an actor: I do,
You can't expect me to not-do,
Unsay,
Non-move.
Once you've got me out here in front of
God and the critics and everybody,
How am I supposed to get transparent
For half a minute, for God's sake?
So go inward, somebody says.
No, thanks, that's a lonely
Scary journey back inward
Down
Back into the
Hollow

Spaces

between

REACHING FAUST

This is what I learned
From playing Faust:
The trembling of fingers.
I didn't know that before.

From Faust I learned
That eyes go on searching
After the words
Stop.

The hands of Faust
Reach out to take,
To take from, to take in,
To take back
Whatever the eyes find.

The shoulders hold back.
From those stretched muscles
Comes the rage.

HAVE A HEART OF GOLD

Never hiss the villain
If you're the villain.
Make him human, even soft.
Search for your own villain causes,
Find your fabricated reasons:
Maybe you give to charity,
Or you love your mother,
Or a cat.
You must have at least
Good intentions, please:
True, you're twisting the heroine's arm,
But to save her from the greater pain
Of going against her best interests,
And it's only her left arm,
And I can stop anytime I have to,
And a sore arm's milder than the
Gouging she gave me,
And I will break it, if I need to . . .

THE POET JONATHAN COFFIN, NINETY-SEVEN YEARS YOUNG

At each rehearsal I smell the decay
Of myself, the muscle tone giving
At arch, at instep, ankle, one day the knees,
The thighs the next, the hands will not grip,
And then the diaphragm,
The voice flutters,
I am old, I am
Old, old.

And
Before I can
Resume my
Self
After the two hours' turmoil,
I enter,
Query,
Sleep,
Forget
(If I can remember to),
And float out on my voice into my moment:
      the poet's last act,
      the throat's last urge,
      the heart's last beat.

In the dressing room my muscles pull back together,
Then I am I
And he was he.

DOES THERSITES HAVE A HUMP?

The problem is knowing too much.
Homer gave him a hump and Odysseus
To clapper-claw it with a scepter.
Homer wrung his spine askew
Skewered on a splintered soul.
Shakespeare gave him only
A high moral standard,
Enough hump for Shakespeare.

How much of my self can I strip away?
How much hump can I do without?
Without a trembling ankle,
An angled elbow,
A stammer,
To bare outrage?

DIRECTOR'S PROLOGUE — "TORTESA, THE USURER"

Where do we start--with the playwright, Jacksonian
anglophile, Shakespeare-idolator? Roles? these
gaudy and garrulous Renaissance Florentines?
Meter? ascending from street-corner prose to the

clouds of abstraction? Such headaches and time-place
tangles!
       So here's what you do: Find some architects'
drawings and move in their rooms to define space
marble-floored, hard on the heels. Go from artworks to

underwear. Where does it bind? Let it guide you.
Empty your ears and hear their musicians.
Dance to these centuries' rhythms inside you--
twentieth, fourteenth, nineteenth. Confusion!

Then you'll be ready. Forget facts, intuit.
Bowels and heartbeats will guide you. Just do it.

IN REHEARSAL

An Actor in Five Scenes

1
The First Day -- Enter the Actors

We arrive
as skittish as cold colts
as kissy as maiden aunts
as noisy as a Little League team:
let no one know
how we hurt
to lift this new play
to life
today
knowing how we will make it
stammer and mumble.
Bob, the stage manager, knows:
he passes out the health insurance cards.
We sign.
The day has begun
auspiciously.
I remember my name.
I was given a simple task.
Thank you.

2
Memorizing Lines

I know I must say,
Goodbye till the sunset and I cannot longer . . .
<u>Wrong.</u>

Goodbye till the sunset. And I cannot, longer than I . . .
<u>Doesn't make sense.</u>

I know. I must say
Goodbye till the sunset, and I cannot. Longer than I . . .
<u>Stupid playwright.</u>

I know I must. Say
Goodbye till the sunset. And I cannot longer than . . .
cannot longer. . .
I cannot
<u>do this</u>
<u>any</u>
<u>more</u>
<u>I think</u>
<u>I've begun</u>
<u>to</u>
<u>atro</u>
<u>phy.</u>

3
Halfway Measures

Step one is faith
in process.
Paper cups
on a card table,
three mismatched chairs,
actors in dungarees:
progress
halfway
to a drawing room comedy.
In this room
we daydream
paper cups to china,
plastic to silver,
sweatshirts to morning coats,
like children
whose wish
is will
is belief.
This is a rehearsal.
Decor comes later.
First comes faith.

4
Give and Take

By turns
a look and a glance,
shoulder and hand
alternately,
a laugh and a chuckle,
pause and reply,
insight and comment,
body and body
alternating
back and forth
words to words,
hers to mine,
we give, we take.
Emphasis,
the director calls it
with his hard habit
of naming
things still growing,
impossible to name:
our going out
and coming back,
myself on stage
with the actress,
two things unconscious
while alive,
becoming the two sides
of one heartbeat.

5
Act Three -- The Silence

At every performance
we'll have to earn our way
to this third act
hush and lull.
I've started sweating
off stage
as well as here
in reality.
I've started emptying
to become
someone else
I care about,
so that we can turmoil
she and I
throat-aching after wonder
hacking, holding, halving each other
peering into the silent horror of each other
on the way to peace.

ADDENDUM

"In Rehearsal" was the final poem in the manuscript Warren Kliewer left behind. The two following this page surfaced after his death.

THE LAST ACT ON LATE NIGHT VAUDEVILLE

The headliner fizzled.
The audience booed running out,
all but these sleepy stragglers.
I wanted my money's worth.
I got it:
"Carlos Antonio,
Master of Conundrums and Mysteries."
Black hair slicked straight back,
big white teeth gleaming,
suavely smoothing a fold
of his black-trimmed
burgundy silk jacket.
"Yes, I am the Power of the Universe.
Did you rubes expect me
to have fangs and breathe fire?"
He displays a ten-inch ticking watch.
"Listen. Listen.
Count the seconds beginning ... now. "
Rubes do as told. We count:
fifty-six, fifty-seven, fifty-eight,
and on fifty-nine, the bell rings.
"I have just removed one second
from the history of the universe."
I alone applaud his slight bow,
afraid not to.
It was a trick watch, of course.
But suppose it wasn't.
How many creatures destined
to be conceived that second
were never born?
How many people ready to find love
in a chance meeting with a stranger
are still alone?
Is it true a dead volcano in New Mexico
erupted this morning?
No, it was a trick watch,
never mind the snowstorm in Israel
and the flowers blooming in March
in Minnesota.

THE FORMER DJ OF "THE EARLY SHOW"

My friend Richard
took the 6 o'clock
up-and-at-'em-music
and slick-staccato-talk show.
"Get the people up to work,"
ran the station manager's formula,
"and clock them in on time."
Dick fast-talked his way
through September,
in October
had dreams about his
weary listeners,
murmured in November,
his lips kissing the microphone:
pull it up
that blanket
up around your ears
rain's in the forecast
twenty degrees and going down
do you really like your job
come on, another five minutes
your boss is sleeping in today
lie back and listen
to these soothing strings

Now there's a new DJ,
used to be an
auctioneer.
Unemployment in the county
has gone down,
the divorce rate
back up.

ACKNOWLEDGMENTS

Grateful acknowledgement for permission to reprint these poems is made to the editors of *Cincinnati Poetry Review, Commonweal, Descant, The Dramatists Guild Quarterly, Exchange: A Journal of Opinion for the Performing Arts, Journal of New Jersey Poets, Kansas Quarterly, Mennonite Life,* and *South Dakota Review*, who first included these poems in their publications.

Photos of Warren Kliewer on the cover and page xv, courtesy of the National Portrait Gallery (Washington, D.C.).

For more information about Warren Kliewer and his work:
http://www.warrenkliewer.com

Warren Kliewer (1931-1998) was a playwright first, director second,
actor third, as well as professor and producer. Author of over 40
plays, he co-edited the 7-volume series, *Religious Theatre* (1964-1971)
and contributed scholarly essays throughout his career including a
chapter on 'Directors and Direction,' in *The Cambridge History of
American Theatre*, vol. 2 (1999).

Born into a Mennonite community in Mountain Lake,
Minnesota, Warren studied English and Theatre Arts at the
universities of Kansas and Minnesota, respectively, earning an MA at
the former and MFA at the latter; then teaching both subjects at
colleges and universities in Indiana and Kansas, 1959-1969. His
directorial roles, along with his literary output — nearly twenty plays
within one decade — led him away from teaching and into a career
of acting roles on stage and screen. He held a range of professional
roles in theater, centered mostly in New Jersey and New York City,
where he remained for the rest of his life, with his wife, an actress and
literary professional, Michèle LaRue.

In 1976, he became a member of The New Dramatists in New

York, where his plays *The Booth Brothers* and *The Berserkers* were produced in 1977 and 1978, respectively. After his departure from academic roles, he dealt less with his religious heritage, although principles of pacifism and social justice remained at the heart of his work, as he shifted to figures and events in the history of American democratic and social reform. To this end, Kliewer also wrote essays in literary criticism, theatre studies and folklore studies, assessing the role of literature and contemporary dramatic culture as an engine for identity formation, social critique and political change.

Previous collections of his poetry and plays include: *Red Rose and Gray Cowl*, 1960; *Moralities and Miracles*, 1962; *Liturgies, Games, Farewells*, 1974. His novel *The Violators* (1964), examines tensions and contradictions in a fictional, separatist religious community, which reflect those he perceived in his own heritage. Other contributions include "A Bird in the Bush," an opera libretto with music composed by Herbert Bielawa (1962), and his musical *A Lean and Hungry Priest* (music by Dan Newmark) was produced in Los Angeles in 1973.

Stage acting roles included:

(New York) Alexander Hamilton, *Aaron Burr*; Legendre/General Dillon, *Danton's Death*; Cutbeard, *Epicoene*, 1975; Witness #1, *The Investigation*, 1980;

(Regional) Bishop of Lax, *See How They Run* and *Pool's Paradise*; First Guard/Chorus, *Antigone*; Henry Peabody, *Tobacco Road*, Fulton Opera House, 1975; Reverend John Hale, *The Crucible*, Fulton Opera House, 1975; Dr. Bonfant, *The Waltz of the Toreadors*, New Jersey Shakespeare Festival, 1980;

(Stock) Queeg, *Caine Mutiny Court Martial*; Gordon Lowther, *The Prime of Miss Jean Brodie*; Keller, *The Miracle Worker*; Gordon Miller, *Room Service*.

Major tours, including one-man shows: Dr. Mayberry, *I Never Sang for My Father*; Judge/Major, *Inherit the Wind; Faustus; The Seven Ages of an American; Dissenters, Uncle Dan's Financial Tips*.

Screen appearances include the films: *Ragtime; Svengali*, and television: *The Adams Chronicles*.

See further tributes on his life in, Elmer F. Suderman, "Warren Kliewer: Writer and Mennonite." *Mennonite Life* 53.4 (December 1998): 8; Dallas Wiebe, "An Elegy for Warren Kliewer." *Mennonite Life* 53.4 (December 1998): 9; Lauren Friesen, "Tribute to Warren Kliewer." *Mennonite Quarterly Review* 72.4 (1998): 691-92; Raylene Hinz-Penner, "For Warren Kliewer." *Mennonite Life* 53.4 (December 1998): 7.

www.ingramcontent.com/pod-product-compliance
Lightning Source LLC
Chambersburg PA
CBHW030513130626
46549CB00007B/2968